'Sustaining grace is the m
that spirit Jeremy address
again!'

Geoff Thomas, author and speaker

'Jeremy Walker's book should be sent to every Christian church for their thoughtful reflection. Jeremy writes with both the insights of a pastor and a man who has a care and concern for the cause of the gospel. It would be a huge mistake to think that Providing for Pastors is simply a pep talk for congregations rightly to remunerate their pastors. How a congregation cares for its pastor(s) will indicate how deeply the gospel of the grace of God has sunk into the lifeblood of that congregation. I recommend this little book unreservedly. '

Ian Hamilton, Editor, Banner of Truth Magazine

'Finances are a subject that Christians often shy away from. Yet the Bible has a great deal to say about how we use our money. Jeremy Walker has addressed this topic head-on, providing a biblical and practical introduction to how churches and individual believers should approach the subject. His focus on the pressing matter of pastoral remuneration is perhaps especially necessary. The book will be useful to church officers considering their church's approach to finances as well as to individual believers thinking about how they use their money.'

Robert Strivens, pastor, Bradford on Avon Baptist Church

'In Providing For Pastors, Jeremy Walker contributes much-needed guidance on a topic that often proves difficult to navigate. He uses biblical principles to emphasize and encourage the importance of churches caring for their pastors. With clear instruction and application of these principles, Pastor Walker shows church members how to provide for their under-shepherds in a way that honors God. May the Kingdom of Christ expand as God raises up pastors, as their churches provide for them, and as God uses this resource to aid in that.'

Anthony Mathenia, pastor, Christ Church, New River Valley, Virginia

Providing for Pastors

Providing for Pastors

Jeremy Walker

EP BOOKS

(Evangelical Press) Unit C, Tomlinson Road, Leyland, PR25 2DY, England

epbooks.org
e-mail: sales@epbooks.org

First published in Great Britain in 2023

British Library Cataloguing in Publication Data

A record for this book is available from the British Library

ISBN 978–1–78397–350–7

Designed by Jordan Cox

Printed in the UK

Contents

Introduction 9
1. The principle of giving 11
2. The priority in giving 16
3. Providing for pastors 23
4. Teaching this truth 41
5. Some practical principles and patterns 54
6. Thinking more widely 73

Introduction

Christians give. It is one of the instincts of the redeemed heart. They give of themselves—their time and their energy. They give of their substance—their money and their things. That generous instinct arises from a heart made new after the image of God in Christ, a heart eagerly disposed to give sacrificially for the sake of others. When the apostle Paul wants to encourage God's people to be faithful, generous, ready givers, he points them back to Christ Jesus: 'For you know the grace of our Lord Jesus Christ, that though He was rich, yet for your sakes He became poor, that you through His poverty might become rich' (2 Cor. 8:9).

The Christian is also called to be a wise steward. Even though he who gives is to give with liberality

(Rom. 12:8), all those who receive a gift from God are to minister that gift to one another 'as good stewards of the manifold grace of God' (1 Pet. 4:10). Every Christian is to be a good steward who is both wise and faithful (Luke 12:42; 1 Cor. 4:2).

As believers, we ought to be primed to give our time, our energy, our money—whatever resources are at our disposal—for the work of the Lord, for the health of his kingdom. But what does that actually look like?

1
The principle of giving

Primarily, a Christian's giving means giving to the local church of which you are a committed member. The church is the one institution with direct divine sanction for the work of Christ's kingdom. It is the one missionary organisation with a heavenly mandate. It is the one establishment with a celestial constitution. Its work is defined by divine fiat—that is, God himself has spoken with authority concerning the church's identity and activity. It is the one body with a guarantee of perpetual existence and unending profitable service. It is also the one organisation which has the primary and legitimate claim on our financial contributions to the kingdom of God.

I appreciate that true believers may have different

convictions about the nature and function of the church, but the principles are plain. My convictions manifestly inform what follows, but I trust that the principles can be taken and applied righteously in various contexts, whatever the specific practice of them.

Giving to the local church

It is clear from the Scriptures that Christians should support the work of the Lord by systematic and proportionate giving made through the local church (Mal. 3:8–10; 1 Cor. 16:1–2; 2 Cor. 8 and 9). Whether or not you take formal tithing[1] as a helpful principle, it is certainly indicative of the attitude of God's people concerning giving to God's kingdom. And what of gifts and offerings made according to one's ability and willingness of heart (Gen. 14:18–20; Ex. 36:2–7; 2 Cor. 8:1–5)? There is no blessing from God, perhaps directly through the church and its ministry, for which an offering of thanksgiving might not form part of an appropriate response. The true principle of giving in the new covenant is for someone to do so 'as he may prosper' (1 Cor. 16:2). This is a grateful generosity in which giving is the instinctive and cheerful response of the one who has himself received all things, not least salvation, as a free gift (1 Cor. 4:7). Such giving is not a

---

1 Tithing is the setting apart of one tenth of one's income for investment in the kingdom of God.

civil or ecclesiastical tax, nor is it the responsibility of any civil or ecclesiastical authority to elicit a payment by edict, threat or force. The only obligation here is the obligation of the renewed and instructed heart. Any necessary administration in the matter is primarily the administration of the local church.

It is true that there are other institutions, organisations and associations besides the local church which are doing fine work. Many of them are doing work that lies outside the proper remit of the church. These too might deserve your time, attention and support. Some of them do not have the capacity or desire, or even the need, to clamour for your probably hard-earned cash. Some of them are known to thousands, some to few. Some of them are eminently worthy, others debatably so. You may certainly consider supporting them financially, if you are able. I also understand that there are some avenues of genuine Christian service that are difficult to define in terms of the role of the church either as the direct instigator or overseer.

But that is not the question here. Our question is, 'What should be my priority in giving?' The answer is that the first call on your financial investment ought to be the church to which you belong. That particular local church is particularly called to engage locally in the work to which the whole church of Christ, more generally considered, is called. Do not divert your investment from the body constituted and instituted by the Lord by giving to other bodies of human invention which are seeking to replicate that work. If you trust the elders and the deacons (one presumes that you do, if you belong to the church), and if they have a sincere and wise desire for kingdom investment (and they ought to have such a desire), and if you have a little extra that you wish to give or to do (and many of us have that), why not give a little more to that church of which you are a part? Most church officers and the congregations they serve already know where and how and why they might invest any further funds made available.

Giving to other churches and causes

And what of other churches? Do you know of congregations that are seeking to support missionaries, or plant churches, or erect or purchase buildings? Are there churches that struggle to support their pastors? If you have given all that you might and all that you could to your own congregation, might you suggest to the elders and deacons that this could be a worthwhile investment? If your church is already involved in such support, and you have more in your pocket, why not pass it along independently and anonymously?

If, after your righteous investment in Christ's church, you have additional discretionary funds or wish to make further sacrifices to other Christian endeavours, then by all means go ahead. I suggest that—should you feel conscience-bound to make such an investment—you reserve those gifts only for work that lies outside the remit of the church, rather than investing it in something that is replicating or replacing that church work but without a divine mandate. And unless and until you find such a need, then look nearer at hand and, I hope, nearer to heart. Christ loves his church. It was to a church that Paul wrote concerning the grace of our Lord Jesus Christ, 'that though He was rich, yet for your sakes He became poor, that you through His poverty might become rich' (2 Cor. 8:9). It is in and through the local church that the first response to this example ought to be made.

2
The priority in giving

But what ought to be the priority of faithful local churches? The short answer is, the preaching of the Word of God.

The church is ruled by the Lord through his Word, the Scriptures. Therefore, from the first days of the New Testament church in Jerusalem, the prayerful ministry of God's Word was the cornerstone of the life and government of the church. When the focus of the apostles was in danger of being dragged away from this, they called on the church to 'seek out from among you seven men of good reputation, full of the Holy Spirit and wisdom' to take care of other important ministries. 'But,' they said, 'we will give ourselves continually to prayer and to the ministry of the word' (Acts 6:3–4).

The church's highest continuing office has as its unique requirement the ability to teach (1 Tim. 3:2; 5:17). The proclamation of the word of life by a man of prayer is the central function of the church, which is and ought to be the pillar and ground of the truth (1 Tim. 3:15). Even the noble service of the deacons was given in order that prayer and the ministry of the Word of God might not suffer neglect. It was by no means wrong that the widows of Jerusalem should receive proper care, but it was wrong that their care be at the expense of prayer and the ministry of Scripture. Indeed, without the preaching of God's truth, before long the care of the widows would simply wither away. The preaching and teaching of Scripture is God's means to form and to inform his church.

A congregational challenge

This presents a challenge to congregations of all sorts and stages of life as churches. For example, a well-established and well-supported congregation might become entrenched in its regular life, and not pause to consider its opportunities and obligations, simply rolling down the rut of its routines or building a reserve that never gets employed. A dwindling congregation might imagine that it should devote its dwindling resources to the maintenance of a crumbling building, or it might go on investing in places miles away from their own local mission field—the needy community on their immediate doorstep. A younger or newly planted church might invest in its local profile, build its online presence, or imagine that the first priority is to establish themselves in a physical property.

Our spiritual priorities tend to be quickly reflected in our financial priorities. In many cases, the living stones suffer at the expense of some merely material concern. The first concern of any church should be the spiritual health of its members, and that involves the gathering and the feeding of the flock by means of God's Word being proclaimed. So what should we do with our financial firstfruits? We should invest in the preaching of divine truth, and that means supporting pastors and preachers.

Do you only get what you pay for?

Even here, I want to offer an encouragement and a warning. Financial provision for those elders who are rightly entitled to receive it should not be allowed to undermine or discourage the culture of voluntary sacrifice in the church of Jesus Christ. Perhaps some might fall into the trap of thinking, 'If service in the church deserves financial remuneration, then any and all service in the church deserves some kind of financial remuneration.' It is a twisted application of the 'you get what you pay for' principle. This is a false conclusion to draw, and might result in an unhealthy culture of 'necessary reimbursement' displacing a holy culture of 'voluntary sacrifice'.

We must emphasise that this holy culture of voluntary sacrifice should be as marked in the pastors of a church as anyone else, whether or not they are fully financially supported. They are men who shepherd the flock of God which is among them, 'serving as overseers, not by compulsion but willingly, not for dishonest gain but eagerly' (1 Pet. 5:2). They do not serve simply because they are paid. In fact, if anything, pastors ought to be exemplary in their demonstration of this culture of Christlike self-giving. They are not men who count off the minutes until they can lay down their tools. They are not men given to the bare minimum that their wage, meagre or otherwise, might oblige. They do and will, as allowed or required, cheerfully carry out the regular work of any 'ordinary member', without complaining at or resenting it. They might properly be spared some of that, so that they can give themselves to other priorities, but not because they are above it. They readily add whatever else might be required by their office. They follow the Master who took the towel and the bowl and washed the feet of his disciples (John 13:1–17).

In the culture of necessary reimbursement, people might begin to assume that you work when you are paid, and not otherwise. Even in a smaller church, this might result in the mentality that the pastor should do most or even all of the work in the congregation—after all, he is being paid to do so. In a larger, perhaps more affluent congregation, we might end up with the ugly situation of having so many people 'on staff' that no-one else is willing or able to do anything. At the extreme, you may end up with pastors, associate pastors and pastoral assistants, youth pastors and every other imaginable brand of pastors; deacons of all stripes and of none; organists and pianists, worship leaders and worship teams; youth workers and children's workers; caretakers and custodians; secretaries and personal assistants and administrators; and so on and so forth, world without end! And some, if not all of these, are expecting to be paid or expected to be paid. It is not necessarily that such primary and support appointments are wrong. It does not necessarily mean that the church is top-heavy.

However, under such circumstances the pastors of churches can become mere executives, looking for recruits, hiring staff to get certain jobs done. It is a pernicious attitude and it often leads to an unhealthy environment. To be sure, in larger churches there may be real benefit in having not only multiple supported pastors, but also perhaps deacons and others who are paid to help ensure the smooth and orderly running of the church in all aspects of its life. Even so, the church is, at its heart, a voluntary organisation in which 'the whole body, joined and knit together by what every joint supplies, according to the effective working by which every part does its share, causes growth of the body for the edifying of itself in love' (Eph. 4:16). It is not a professional organisation. It is not a band of spectators who pay to watch others perform. Every member should feel the force of the apostle's plea: 'by the mercies of God, that you present your bodies a living sacrifice, holy, acceptable to God, which is your reasonable service' (Rom. 12:1).

No doubt there may be appropriate expressions of gratitude for the service of the saints within and by the church and her individual members, but these should not be considered, given or received as proper payments for services rendered. We do not work for a fading reward, but for an eternal crown, and we run and we wrestle accordingly (1 Cor. 9:24–26). We give not just our money, but our time and our energy and our ability, proving ourselves to be volunteers in the day of Christ's power (Ps. 110:3). Generally speaking, the church and her members ought cheerfully and willingly to take up whatever their hand finds to do as a ready expression of their relation to Christ Jesus:

> Having then gifts differing according to the grace that is given to us, let us use them: if prophecy, let us prophesy in proportion to our faith; or ministry, let us use it in our ministering; he who teaches, in teaching; he who exhorts, in exhortation; he who gives, with liberality; he who leads, with diligence; he who shows mercy, with cheerfulness (Rom. 12:6–8).

3
Providing for pastors

While many churches in many places do make a priority of preaching, and do provide adequately for their pastors, this happy situation is not universal. In addressing this concern, I hope it is clear that I am not criticising those who freely and cheerfully give all they can for the support of the church and her pastors, even if it is not much. Furthermore, many congregations are happily and willingly served by faithful men who would, as Philip Henry said, 'rather preach for nothing than not at all.'[2] Neither am I dealing with the righteous attitude to money that every pastor—and every Christian—must have. The under-shepherds of the flock must be 'not

2 Quoted in John Blanchard, *Gathered Gold* (Welwyn: Evangelical Press, 1984), p. 238.

greedy for money', 'not covetous' (1 Tim. 3:3). Such a man ought to be marked, more and more, by the kind of spirit that enabled Paul to say that 'I have learned in whatever state I am, to be content' (Phil. 4:11).

In addition, I cannot fully address in this short treatment the responsibility of the elders of the flock to give themselves to prayer and to the ministry of the Word, devoting themselves to gathering, guiding, governing and guarding the flock of Christ, as they follow their Master in giving themselves to others. Of necessity, I am having to assume that we are talking about fundamentally faithful and hard-working shepherds of Christ's sheep.

Again, I am not considering the faith of God's people in the Lord's boundless ability to provide. I am not dismissing churches that are not yet in a position to support a preacher, or who are eager to do so but lack a man or men to support in that way.

Worthy of his hire

I am addressing the responsibility of true churches of Jesus Christ to provide financial support for the men who faithfully watch out for their souls, 'as those who must give account' (Heb. 13:17). Any such man is constantly to attend to the service of Christ in the church (1 Tim. 4:15–16; 2 Tim. 4:2): it is the business of his life's energy. He is to minister the Word and to pray, watching for the souls of those entrusted to his care, as one accountable to Jesus Christ at the judgment (2 Tim. 4:1). This is the heavy responsibility of every man called to be an elder, whether he is gifted for the regular public proclamation of the truth or not. It is this labour, diligently conducted, that constitutes the labourer worthy of his hire.

Pastors must be careful here. There are many matters today which easily distract the man of God from his primary responsibility. Our first duty is not to write blogs or books, not to have a popular podcast, not to garner a national or international following, not to be a 'conference preacher', not to have our name in lights on earth, but rather to have a good reputation in the heavenly places for the faithful discharge of our appointed labours. While we must use our gifts in such a way as not to be in danger of having neglected them on Christ's return, we must invest those talents in the spheres to which Christ himself directs us as the Great Shepherd of the sheep.

In carrying out this spiritual warfare, such men should receive the support of the church: 'Who ever goes to war at his own expense? Who plants a vineyard and does not eat of its fruit? Or who tends a flock and does not drink of the milk of the flock?' (1 Cor. 9:7). Such a duty should be one that such a man carries out without being distracted by other cares: 'No one engaged in warfare entangles himself with the affairs of this life, that he may please him who enlisted him as a soldier' (2 Tim. 2:4). He should be able to give himself entirely to the things to which he is called (1 Tim. 4:15).

It is the responsibility of the whole church, with her officers, to take account of the demands of the office. If that work is initially small, then proper financial support will enable him, under God, to enlarge it. The man of God should set out to expand the sphere of his usefulness, not only within the congregation, which he hopes might grow, but by preaching around and about, to make known the gospel of Christ. The church should liberate its pastor-preachers to preach and to shepherd.

An old question

This question of providing for pastors is not a new matter. In the 1680s, the introduction to a book entitled *The Gospel Minister's Maintenance Vindicated* included these words:

> ... fearing some Congregations have not duly weighed and considered, of their indispensible Duty to the Ministry; in respect of providing such a Maintenance, for those who Labour amongst them, and are over them in the Lord, as they ought to do, by which means (it may be

> feared that) many of them may be hindered or obstructed in attending on their Work, in serving of Christ and his People, as the Nature of their sacred Imployment and Office requires, and the present Day especially calls for, and as the Lord himself hath also Ordained.[3]

Demonstrating a similar estimate of the importance of this matter, the Baptists' 'second London' *Confession of Faith* of 1677/89 declares that

> 'It is incumbent on the churches to whom [pastors] minister, not only to give them all due respect, but also to communicate to them of all their good things according to their ability, so as they may have a comfortable supply, without being themselves entangled in secular affairs; and may also be capable of exercising hospitality towards others; and this is required by the law of nature, and by the express order of our Lord Jesus, who hath ordained that they that preach the Gospel, should live of the Gospel.[4]

---

3 Introduction to a book attributed to Benjamin Keach, *The Gospel Minister's Maintenance Vindicated* (London: John Harris, 1689). The spelling is original. This has recently been reprinted in James M. Renihan (ed.), *Faith and Life for Baptists: The Documents of the London Particular Baptist General Assemblies, 1689–1694* (Palmdale, CA: RBAP, 2016), p. 143.

4 Chapter 26 ("Of the Church"), paragraph 10. I do not believe that the Westminster Confession has a corresponding passage; Presbyterian subordinate documents sometimes contain direction on this question. The Savoy Declaration, addressing 'The Institution of Churches, and the Order Appointed in Them by Jesus Christ', makes plain that those 'engaged in the work of public preaching ... enjoy the public maintenance upon that account.'

This time-tested Baptist Confession spells out the twofold duty of the church with respect to godly and faithful pastors: respect for the man and provision for the man. The two are yoked together. We might go so far as to say that the church's care for her pastor is a register of her esteem for the man and the ministry he exercises. Tell me what a church pays its pastor, or at least how it approaches the question, and I should be able to estimate their relish for God's truth and its proclamation. A scripturally grounded view of the pastoral office ought to engender right respect and right provision for men holding that office. The church is often hamstrung by the way in which the ministry of the Word is practically despised through churches failing to support—according to scriptural principles—the men appointed to this ministry.

Respect for the man

We might presume from the balance of this paragraph in the Confession that the common problem of our age was equally the case in the seventeenth century: professed respect without adequate provision. The giving of respect seems to be almost assumed, but even this is threatened today. We must remember that pastors are, by Christ's appointment, his servants to govern—by way of biblical instruction and persuasion—the church which he purchased with his own blood.

This is not a lever for pastors to elevate themselves into infallible demagogues and autocrats. They are under-shepherds of Christ's sheep whose duty and accountability to the risen Christ is carefully and vigorously laid out and applied in Scripture. However, it does mean that the radical individualism and proud anti-authority spirit of the age in which we live must be guarded against. (See the instructions to the church in 1 Thessalonians 5:12–13 or Hebrews 13:17, for example, to see that these issues are not restricted to our day.) Elders are men gifted by Christ for understanding and applying the Scriptures as the rule of faith and life, and exercising Christ's rule in Christ's church. If the church does not believe that a man is so gifted, then he should not be recognised; if he is recognised as so gifted, then he should be heard accordingly.

Provision for the man

The second element of corporate responsibility to pastors that the Baptist Confession makes clear is 'to communicate to them of all their good things according to their ability [1 Tim. 5:17; Gal. 6:6–7], so as they may have a comfortable supply, without being themselves entangled in secular affairs [2 Tim. 2:4].' One measure of this support is that—as men having a particular responsibility for the duty of hospitality (expected of all church members, required of elders)—they should be enabled to exercise hospitality towards others (1 Tim. 3:2). The pastor's open heart should prompt an open hand; the church ensures that the extended hand is well supplied.

This duty of providing materially for the minister of God's Word is required by the law of nature, and by the express order of our Lord Jesus, who has ordained that those who preach the gospel should live from the gospel (1 Tim. 5:18; 1 Cor. 9:6–14). Three key passages address the matter of ministerial maintenance.

1 Timothy 5:17 speaks of 'double honour'. From the context of the New Testament as a whole (compare Matt. 27:6–9; Acts 4:34; 5:2–3; 7:16) and 1 Timothy 5 itself (see vv. 3–8, 16), it is clear that this has primary reference to financial support, although it does not exclude well-earned respect. In this case, 'double' (compare Rev. 18:6; Matt. 23:15) 'figuratively indicates amplitude or great extent. Double honour, then, is ample material or financial support.'[5] It does not simply mean 'double the salary of this or that other man'. Such honour is to be focused on those who labour in the word and doctrine. It is extended—where necessity and capability provide—to all those who rule well, irrespective of their

5 Sam Waldron, *A Modern Exposition of the 1689 Baptist Confession of Faith* (Darlington: Evangelical Press, 1995), p. 325.

particular gift and sphere of labour. If those who rule *well* are worthy of *double* honour, then *all* those ruling must be worthy of *reasonable* honour.

Galatians 6:6 requires the sharing of 'good things with him who teaches', and these things are clearly material (v. 10). The direction is specific: a Christian's good things in this world are to be shared with the one who teaches that Christian the Word of God. It is a principle of righteous returns: having received the teaching, we respond with care for the one who teaches. 'Those who highly value the labour of the servant of God will find themselves blessed with highly valuable labour.'[6] How often, and how sadly, the church gets only what she pays for.

1 Corinthians 9:14 effectively describes material support as 'a living'. The one who preaches the gospel should enjoy—as the reward of his labours—a sufficiency of the world's goods. 1 Peter 5:2 and 1 Timothy 6:5 seem to suggest that the generous New Testament church needed particularly to guard against charlatans who sought to line their own pockets by entering the ministry. In some circles, few would be tempted into the gospel ministry by the potential financial rewards!

It is worth noting, further, that this is not a matter

6 Waldron, p. 325.

of mere charity. Benjamin Keach is plain: 'It is not (as one well observes) your Charity that we ask for them, but Justice and Right, which the very Light of Nature as well as God's Word clearly sheweth.'[7] No congregation or member should look upon any minister as a 'charity case', nor should he expect to feel like one. The minister's financial support is not an act of mercy but of justice. No member should imagine that they individually, or the congregation as a whole, deserve particular plaudits for the generous support of their pastor. It is his right—his just entitlement!

Working man, working wage

There ought to be a legitimate connection between the working man and his working wage. In some cases, the church may not be able to pay the wage it might wish. In some environments, there may even be some government benefits that are available to families whose income is below an appropriate level. However, no faithful church should be assuming that the government will make up what is lacking in their support of elders or other salaried workers.

If it is good to labour, working with your hands that you 'may have something to give him who has

7 Keach, 'The Gospel Minister's Maintenance Vindicated', in Renihan (ed.), *Faith and Life for Baptists*, p. 164.

need' (Eph. 4:28), and if 'the labourer is worthy of his wages' (1 Tim. 5:18), and if a man who does not work should not eat (2 Thes. 3:10), then the aim of the church should always be to ensure that the pastor is not a burden on the state (Prov. 3:27). Certainly, it should never be the plan to oblige the civil authority to supplement or subsidise the church's support of its pastor. I acknowledge that a man is entitled to take that to which he is entitled in state benefits (for example, any tax rebates, allowances and so on). However, while in some cases a man or a church may be entitled (for example, in the case of disability) or obliged (where the church's funds fall below the level at which they can properly support a man) to receive state benefits, that principle of righteous returns forbids that it should ever be assumed or pursued.

The same holds good at the other end of the scale. Even should a minister have some private means, the principle and practice of the congregation supporting him is just and right—the labourer is still worthy of his hire. Such an attitude and activity establishes a righteous pattern and sets a good example. What such a minister does with that support is his business. He might choose to return it to the church, or lay it out in some distinct work of ministry or charity or hospitality.

Whatever the case, no pastor seeking to be a good

soldier and 'engaged in warfare' should need to be entangled 'with the affairs of this life' (2 Tim. 2:3–4). He should not be distracted by worldly needs, but rather be amply supplied by the church, for his good and their own. Besides, if he is a man of the character Christ requires ('not greedy for money'), there is a sense in which he cannot have too much: he will use it wisely and generously, and furthermore will answer to Christ himself for the use or abuse of his worldly goods.

It is clear from other Scriptures that pastors in the local church are entitled to material support. Christopher Wright reminds us that—while elders are not priests in the distinctive way that was true of the tribe of Levi—in ancient Israel the Levites were deliberately consigned to landlessness; they were never expected to possess economic power with all its concomitants. But they were not consigned to poverty:

> dependence on an obedient people should have meant perfectly adequate provision for their material needs, just as Israel's dependence on their faithful God would include full provision. The principle that those who serve God and teach God's people should be fully provided for by God's people is emphatically reapplied in the N[ew] T[estament]. Galatians 6:6 applies it to Christian teachers (cf. 1 Tim. 5:17f.). Paul actually makes reference to

> O[ld] T[estament] priestly dues, along with many other supporting arguments (including another Deuteronomic law, 25:4, and a command of Christ), in establishing the responsibility of Christian churches to provide for the material needs of those who work for the cause of the Gospel (1 Cor. 9:13). Paul had freely chosen to waive this right in his own personal case, but he explicitly makes himself an exception to the principle he insists on for others. Unfortunately, some Christian organizations have turned Paul's exception, rather than his rule, into a policy imposed on their workers. But in view of the teaching of both OT and NT, churches or other Christian groups that fail to pay their workers adequate living wages are not 'living by faith,' but are simply living in disobedience.[8]

Note Wright's close connection of the Old Testament pattern with the New Testament application. We also see this in 1 Corinthians 9:13: 'Do you not know that those who minister the holy things eat of the things of the temple, and those who serve at the altar partake of the offerings of the altar?' Those whose main business is the holy things of the new covenant are entitled to obtain support accordingly.

---

8 Christopher Wright, *New International Biblical Commentary on Deuteronomy* (Ada, MI: Baker Books, 2012), pp. 215–216.

Generous care

The particular focus of such adequate provision is those men who are called to and who excel in the public ministry of the Word of God. The level of material support enjoyed by these men should be generous and ample. A forerunner of the Puritans, William Perkins, underscores the issue. He was troubled by 'the inadequacy of the financial recompense and status given to those who enter this calling.' He reminds us that

> all men are flesh and blood. In that respect they must be allured and won to embrace this vocation by the kind of arguments which may well persuade flesh and blood.... especially now, under the gospel, the ministerial calling is poorly provided for, even although it deserves to be rewarded most of all. Certainly it would be an honourable Christian policy to make at least good provision for this calling, so that men of the worthiest gifts might be won for it.

It is not an argument to put a carnal bait before men, but rather a recognition that there will be a real effect when the ministry of God's Word 'yields nothing but a clear road to poverty.' For many men, the call to the ministry is a call to poverty, and that ought never to be carelessly assumed or casually allowed. Perkins says,

> unless special attention is given to this matter, it will

be left unreformed. No doubt, in the Old Testament period, if God himself had not given direct orders for the material support of the Levites, they would have suffered the same privation as the ministry does today. These considerations, taken together, produce an infallible argument. For who will accept such vile contempt and such a weighty responsibility for no reward? But where there is so much contempt and such a heavy burden, yet such a poor reward, is it any wonder that a good minister is one in a thousand?[9]

Setting a salary

With this in mind, pastoral salaries should not necessarily be fixed to another pay scale (however generous), although in some cases it may be useful to think of what other 'professionals' receive, at least as a starting point. Neither should those pastoral salaries simply be calculated as a rough average of the congregational wage (any more than that they should necessarily and automatically keep him well above or below it). Such salaries ought to be a principled recognition of the worth of the office, and the earned esteem of the man holding it.

Without the faithful ministry of God's Word, the church is a hollow shell, and will slowly shrivel from

9 William Perkins, *The Art of Prophesying* (Edinburgh: Banner of Truth, 1996), pp. 95–96.

within. This makes the provision and support of faithful ministry the church's financial priority. Each church must consider a man's righteous entitlement against their capacity to provide for him, and the principle of righteously and generously rewarding exemplary, faithful, fruitful service. The Puritan Thomas Watson goes so far as to connect reticence in this matter to hypocrisy:

> the hypocrite's desires are cheap; he would have spiritual things, but he will be at no charges for them; he cares not how much money he parts with for his lusts; he hath money to spend upon a drunken companion, but he hath no money to part with for the maintaining of God's ordinances; hypocrites cry up religion, but cry down maintenance of ministers. But true desires are costly; David would not offer burnt-offerings without cost, 1 Chron. 21:24. An hungry man will give any thing for food; as it fell out in the siege of Samaria, 2 Kings 6:25. That man did never hunger after Christ, who thinks much of parting with a little silver for the pearl of price.[10]

By contrast, the upright man is 'liberal and communicative':

> he hath a liberal heart towards the maintenance of God's

10 Thomas Watson, 'Discourses upon Christ's Sermon on the Mount', in *Discourses on Important and Interesting Subjects, Being the Select Works of the Rev. Thomas Watson* (Edinburgh; Glasgow: Blackie, Fullarton, & Co.; A. Fullarton & Co., 1829), 2:177.

> worship. He will not let the fire of God's altar go out for want of pouring on a little oil; what vast sums of gold and silver did David prepare for the house of God! 1 Chron. 29:3. 'Moreover, because I have set my affection to the house of my God, I have of my own proper good, of gold and silver, which I have given to the house of my God, over and above all that I have prepared for the holy house, even three thousand talents of gold, of the gold of Ophir, and seven thousand talents of refined silver, to overlay the walls of the houses withal,' &c. Hypocrites, if they may have golden purses, are content to have wooden priests. They love a cheap gospel, they are loath to be put to too much charges. How many have lost their souls to save charges! The upright christian will not offer that to God which costs him nothing.[11]

My aim in so writing is not to stir up frustration among God's people, discontent in a pastor's heart, or tension between the sheep and their under-shepherd. I am concerned for the honour of Christ in his church. How we provide for gospel ministers is an indisputable register of our esteem for the gospel ministry. What message does a pastor's salary send to the church, to the world and to potential gospel ministers about your estimation of his person

11 Thomas Watson, 'The Upright Man's Character', in *Discourses on Important and Interesting Subjects, Being the Select Works of the Rev. Thomas Watson* (Edinburgh; Glasgow: Blackie, Fullarton, & Co.; A. Fullarton & Co., 1829), 1:339.

and work? What message does it send to pastors themselves? Are you declaring to all who care to look that to preach God's Word is a worthless thing to be lightly esteemed, or a worthy calling to be highly esteemed?

4
Teaching this truth

As I trust is clear, providing for pastors is a simple matter of obedience to Christ in his Word. However, it is one of those many commands given which must be taught in accordance with Christ's authority and in anticipation of his presence with us (Matt. 28:20). And there is no doubt that it is the responsibility of the elders to teach these things. However, it might also, under some circumstances, be appropriate for others to assist in the matter.

Self-service?

Someone might object that the responsibility of the elders to address this automatically introduces a problem. How should a pastor deal with this matter without seeming to be self-serving? Will he not immediately open himself up to charges that he is greedy?

Undoubtedly, if he is to address the matter of giving generally, and of pastoral financial support specifically, it is important that the man of God search his own heart to discover his own motives. He must be confident before God and men that he is not feathering his own nest. He must be able to say with Paul that he does not preach the gospel as 'a cloak for covetousness—God is witness' (1 Thes. 2:5).

At the same time, if the pastor has been righteously appointed to his office, he should be a man who is manifestly blameless (1 Tim. 3:2; Tit. 1:6–7). A specific aspect of that blamelessness lies in his attitude to money: he is not to be 'greedy for money' (1 Tim. 3:3; Tit. 1:7). In other words, there should already be a well-grounded assumption in the hearts of the people to whom he preaches that he is not marked by a mercenary spirit, that he is no hireling (John 10:12–13).

Furthermore, there ought to be no instinct for suspicion in the congregation of a faithful man. No congregation is to 'receive an accusation against an elder except from two or three witnesses' (1 Tim. 5:19). They are clearly not to have a sceptical spirit with regard to their ministers and the ministry they receive (and the fact that the whole congregation heard the sermons does not constitute them witnesses to the sin if there was no sin involved!). The spirit of the noble Bereans was to receive the Word readily and also to search the Scriptures where they would find confirmation of what they heard (Acts 17:11). Churches need to understand that it is good to pray that the Lord of the harvest will send labourers into the harvest field. Congregations need to grasp that it is a blessing to enjoy the ministry of such a labourer. They need also to know that the Lord of the harvest has appointed that 'those who preach the gospel should live from the gospel' (1 Cor. 9:14). That lays an obligation upon those churches.

Speaking to the issue

So, typically, the pastor should be free to address this matter as it is necessary and appropriate. He can do this in a variety of ways. First of all, as should be clear, the Scriptures speak to this issue again and again, both directly and indirectly. It is part of a preacher's duty to make this known, not shunning 'to declare to you the whole counsel of God' (Acts 20:27). If a pastor is teaching systematically through the Bible, he will surely come to this as he does so, perhaps almost incidentally and occasionally. When he does so, he should explain and apply these principles without embarrassment. It is what the Word of God says.

It may also become necessary to teach and preach on this more directly, to instruct deliberately and topically. No-one in their right mind is eager to be involved in the kind of church where every sermon includes a call to give more, then to give again, along the lines of a 'health, wealth and prosperity' approach. However, it would not be wrong, from time to time, to deal with this.

A series on giving, rooted in the work of the Lord Christ, could and perhaps should properly take up the matter of how funds received are disbursed, including financial support for pastors. Teaching about the church and her life, or the ministry and its work, could properly address this matter. Pastoral support is one of the demands on the finances of the church. Again, without embarrassment or over-sensitivity, the pastors of a church must deal with this.

Dealing with difficulties

There are further ways to guard against even the appearance of evil. In a church with a healthy eldership, it may be that one of the elders who does not receive much or any financial support might address the matter publicly, rather than a brother who is being fully supported. It might be appropriate for the primary preacher and teacher to address the matter with other elders or the deacons before bringing it to the church, securing the intelligent understanding and commitment of his fellow officers. (I would not necessarily recommend working round individual members of the congregation to address this matter, although it may be appropriate to answer questions or deal with problems in this way. Such an approach may appear manipulative or underhanded, or seem like a series of complaints.)

One difficulty in some churches may be that there is one individual, or a small group of people, who supply most of the money for the church. The temptation might be to focus on them, especially if they are in the horrible habit of assuming that with their giving comes an inordinate control over spending. In effect, some ministers may be held hostage by a wealthy member or members. Too many independent churches end up with a system resembling Anglicanism at its historical worst, where a wealthy member essentially has the church as a 'living' which he dispenses to the man of his choosing. Funds given to the church ought to become the funds of the church, to be employed in accordance with the principles and patterns that govern ecclesiastical finance, and not as a personal fiefdom.

In this respect, we cannot and should not say that it is wrong to give personal gifts to pastors. At the same time, it would be dangerous were such generosity to be or become (or *be seen* to be or become) a means of influence over the elders. The love of money is the 'root of all kinds of evil' (1 Tim. 6:10) and pastors are not immune to its more subtle or cruder enticements. All appearance and reality of personal patronage or possible bribery must be excluded. No elder must ever feel unrighteously beholden to a member of the church, beyond the ordinary expressions of brotherly affection that are proper among fellow members. The pastors must not feel that they must trim their sails in order to avoid running aground on the displeasure of this or that wealthier member or generous 'friend'.

Should there be a particular need, it may be possible for a generous individual to pass on a gift anonymously through the church or a trusted intermediary, such as one of the deacons. Whether or not that is possible, any such gifts should manifestly arrive with 'no strings attached'. If there are such, or even if a pastor feels himself bound by such, then he might need gratefully and graciously to decline the gift. He must not be constrained by the fear of men.

Bear in mind, too, that in a healthy church the deacons are likely to have a particular role in both managing and modelling good, biblical practice. Again, this is not the time to unpack the office and work of the diaconate, but we must always remember that the deacons are not running a business, nor managing a going concern, but serving in a kingdom of which Christ is King. They are not the employers of the pastor, acting as an executive board (neither, for that matter, are they the elders' employees). The deacons must not hire and fire at will, nor are they, individually or together, the sole authority over the finances of the church. Those priorities ought to be set by the elders, not without diaconal input, but neither finally constrained by it. How important is a healthy biblical ecclesiology at such times! We need a solid doctrine of the church with all its proper pieces in place.

The poor pastor

Let me also confess that there will be times when a minister suffers, perhaps with his family, and does so silently and humbly. Perhaps he has inherited an historical mess from the recent past. He has now instructed but he will not arrogantly demand. He has preached but he will not aggressively insist. It may be that, despite his best and wisest efforts, those who pay his wages will not (we will look at the 'cannot' below) respond righteously to his legitimate needs as a man and perhaps as a husband and father, as well as a pastor.

To such brothers, I say with genuine sympathy that there is a good and great Shepherd of the sheep who knows the particular needs of each of his flock. It is not mere pietism to say that he can and does provide. It is not vindictiveness to say that the Lord might remove his servant from a sphere in which he is being neglected by the people for whom he cares, to another sphere in which they will look after him better. It may be that this is one of our Lord's means for working dependence on him in the soul of his child. It may be that he will struggle against poverty all his labouring life in the harvest field before he receives his glorious reward. These are genuine possibilities, and in keeping with the life of the Master he serves (Matt. 8:20) and those who have gone before (Heb. 11:37). There may be times and seasons—long times and painful seasons—in which a servant of the Lord will not quarrel or contend about this, but rather commit himself to him who judges righteously (1 Pet. 2:23), confident that the Judge of all the earth will do right (Gen. 18:25) at the right and proper moment.

But what if there are other difficulties? Are there no other possibilities to address this? What about unusual circumstances? I recall the report of a dear friend, called to preach at a special meeting in a wealthy farming community. As he preached, he had occasion to speak in some way—I do not know how directly—of the duty of the church to care for their pastors in this and other ways. When he had finished preaching, he walked away from the pulpit. As he did so, a man came towards him, plainly agitated and distressed. My friend was taken aback when this man flung himself upon his neck, weeping. The tormented man poured out his tale. He had been the pastor of a church, and among his fellow members and church officers were farmers who would buy the most expensive farming equipment outright, sometimes with cash. He and his family, though, were somewhere close to the breadline, much to the grief of his wife. As I recall the tale, the pastor's wife had once found for him a wonderful coat in a second-hand store in the town, replacing his previous threadbare garment. Delighted with the purchase, the man wore his new coat to church on the next Lord's day. His wife sat in her usual place in the congregation. Behind her, she heard one of the wives of another church officer remark snootily, in a stage whisper, that it appeared that the minister had somehow managed to obtain the cast-off clothes of her own husband that she had given away earlier that week. The cruelty of the whole thing, of which this was a particular instance, broke the mind and heart of that poor man's wife. Whether or not the men and women in the congregation that day heeded the exhortation they heard, I do not know, but it brought home to my friend the seriousness of this matter.

I know of another situation in which a faithful Christian, a financial adviser, offered some helpful counsel to a needy pastor. In doing so, the adviser necessarily became aware of that godly pastor's dire financial circumstances. The Lord had undoubtedly provided for the preacher, but the church had been far from righteous in its dealings with their minister. Appalled, the faithful brother asked privately for a meeting with the deacons of the church, and gave them a blunt assessment of their treatment of the pastor. Those men were probably not deliberately sinning against the pastor. They were largely ignorant, careless and thoughtless, shackled by their failure to consider the truth and the emptiness of the examples that they had seen. It so happened that, at the same time, the preacher in question was preaching through the second letter to the Corinthians and was reaching chapter eight. The faithful financier's counsel coincided with the principled preacher's instruction, and the financial life of the church—not least with regard to pastoral support—was righteously revolutionised.

I do not hold these instances up as absolute models, but I do contend that many ministers might be well-served by a faithful friend of the kinds described above. There may be particular circumstances in which outside counsel or intervention is proper or useful. However it is done, it should always be done graciously and carefully, specifically and helpfully, biblically and practically. Different principles of church government might provide for different mechanisms by which the matter might be addressed. In some cases, certain structures may provide for a regular check on this matter. It may be a sister church who has the opportunity to ask the friendly but searching question. It may be a particular denominational or associational set-up, if you hold to such, whereby there is some forum for making sure that righteousness is being pursued. There may be a suggestion or recommendation of a minimum salary, or a mechanism whereby a shortfall can be made up (without, again, some outside agency being able to hold a church or its pastors to ransom).

Consider the circumstances

In any and every such case, there must be a sensitive appreciation of the particular dynamics of the situation. For example, if the church in question is long-established but poorly instructed, it might be profoundly unhelpful to have someone blunder in from the outside. A measure of credibility must first be established. At some point, though, such counsel, humbly offered, might become necessary.

In the case of a church plant or a pastor-evangelist who is sent out, it is clearly the primary responsibility of a planting church, or a sending church, to undertake the righteous support of him (at least initially) and the proper instruction of any church established. Where several local churches enjoy close communion or good relationships, more or less formally, there is an environment in existence in which this matter can be addressed, as appropriate. Perhaps it is a situation in which an established church seeks advice or assistance from another congregation: that church, or its elders, might properly take up the matter of ministerial financial support as part of their help. The question of more immediate financial investment will be addressed further below.

This matter is clearly addressed in God's Word, and—as a matter of obedience—ought to be carefully considered. Ministers must teach the whole counsel of God, including this. We have something of which to repent if we have not done so. Such teaching should never be and cannot be dismissed as, and ought not to be construed as, an attempt to feather one's own nest or drop less-than-subtle hints. This matter needs to be brought before the church appropriately and in a timely and even regular way, both for the sake of the present elders and for those who will, in due course, follow them. The members of every church must likewise consider whether or not we have served Christ well in this.

Both those in the pulpits and those in the pews must be persuaded of the righteousness of considering and responding to God's Word at this point. Such careful, prayerful thought, with repentance and action where appropriate, and a desire to perform even this for Christ's glory, will promote reformation for the present, and—under God—provide a foundation for the future.

5
Some practical principles and patterns

With regard to working this out practically, I want to develop more fully one or two of the hints and suggestions already made. First of all, it may be that more than one elder could or should be financially supported by the church: 'Let the elders who rule well be counted worthy of double honour, especially those who labour in the word and doctrine. For the Scripture says, "You shall not muzzle an ox while it treads out the grain," and, "The labourer is worthy of his wages"' (1 Tim. 5:17–18).

As already suggested, there are good grounds for considering whether or not any and all elders are entitled to the financial honour that may legitimately be associated with their labours. It is not a demand that all elders must receive some kind of remuneration. However, the time, energy and resources that most elders devote to their labour might properly draw out some kind of response from the church. For example, could each elder have a book budget or an allowance for certain expressions of hospitality or conference attendance? Might they receive some gift of thanks from the congregation as appropriate, even if they do not draw a salary? Might long and faithful service be recognised in some direct and material way?

However, in most instances, the financial support of the church will be primarily focused on a particular man, or a smaller number of men, who give themselves to 'labour in the word and doctrine'. These brothers are what we might call fully vocational pastors—called by the church to serve in a full-time capacity, and financially supported for the purpose of preaching the Word and prayer.

Dealing with discernment

We should not immediately assume that all such elders are entitled to precisely the same salary. That shows a failure to grasp the biblical principles at work with regard both to the pastoral office generally and ministerial support specifically. In many churches, there is a recognition that the elders enjoy a parity of authority. However, that does not and should not necessarily work itself out in parity of remuneration. Such a simplistic conclusion fails to take account of the variety or diversity which is already implied in Paul's language to Timothy.

Some men, says the Scripture, are 'worthy of double honour'. Their first qualification for such honour is not that they have laboured in the Word and doctrine—that simply adds another layer to the consideration. The primary consideration is that they be men who 'rule well'. This seems to suggest the faithful and fruitful discharge of the various functions of their office: it raises questions of integrity, diligence, honesty, length of service, giftedness and usefulness, including perhaps the broader recognition by others of their gifts. Age and experience will probably be factors in the equation, but not the only ones.

Those who are making these assessments—however the church carries out its business—need to be conscious that the man whom Christ has given as a shepherd for his flock is a relatively rare treasure. He is (or they are, however many there may be) given gifts and grace for no less a work than the glorifying of Christ through the calling of sinners to faith and repentance, and the care of repentant believers. He has the duty of ensuring, humanly speaking, that the saints reach heaven by caring for us and guiding us along the way. In other words, he is—or ought to be—an outstanding man, one who would, by diligent application of his God-given gifts, excel in many other possible pursuits and professions. The wage we pay such a man (or such men, if there are more than one) is a demonstration of esteem for his labour, his office and his person. It is an expression (though not the only one) of how we value the ministry of God's Word, and the servant by whom it comes.

The visiting preacher

As an aside, this should also play into any thought given to the compensation offered to visiting preachers, sometimes called an honorarium. I recall a note of appreciation from a well-known British preacher. He wanted to communicate to the church I serve his gratitude that he was, for the first time in a number of months, returning home with sufficient funds not only to cover the costs of his travel to and from his home, but with enough left over to be considered a reasonable recognition of his labours. This was apparently a rare blessing. He would not be the first preacher who has effectively paid for the privilege of preaching to the church which has invited him to do so! This is unconscionable.

On the other hand, I confess that I was recently horrified to discover that some preachers and teachers on the evangelical circuit have a schedule of fees and expenses. If you want them to preach or teach, this is what it will cost: this is how they travel; these are the staff who must travel with them; this is the fee for which they get out of bed; this is the manner in which they must be kept; and so on and so forth. I do not know how this can be defended! In a true pastor, surely it would be reprehensible?

Yes, the labourer is worthy of his hire, and there may be some instances in which, for example, a financial or legal adviser who is working for his living might be obliged to charge for counsel he offers to a church. However, I find it hard to countenance the notion of a genuine ambassador of Christ letting people know how much it will cost them for the privilege of hearing his voice. That is the responsibility of the church to assess, not for the preacher to impose. It smacks of the hireling mentality, or the Corinthian super-apostles with their self-scribed letters of recommendation. Do we charge people to hear the giving of the free offer of the gospel? Such a schedule of fees and charges is not something I imagine the apostle Paul working up! A preacher is certainly free to turn down an invitation if he cannot afford to take it up, or if—for other reasons—he does not believe he will be fairly treated.

And, yes, a visiting preacher is entitled to refuse the honorarium that is offered. I would encourage him not to do so under normal circumstances. He may be in a position where he does not need the money. However, the man who follows him might be in dire straits, and the same recognition of his service would be a real boon to him. What the man who chooses to receive the honorarium does with that money is, again, between him and God. He might give it to someone else, use it for a particular kingdom purpose, contribute it to his own church, or something else. But he should generally accept it, if only for the sake of the next man.

Some pastors make a habit of passing on all gifts received as salaried servants of a given church to the church which pays their salaries. Others have an allowance of sorts for outside preaching, and employ the rewards of those investments as they see fit, before God. Each man in relation to a particular church, and vice versa, might consider how to approach this. We must also take account of those occasions on which a man, or the church which he serves, waives his entitlement or accepts the liabilities because of particular demands or opportunities for investments. Those situations I deal with in greater detail below.

Where visiting preachers are coming in for more intense periods of ministry or for service which required more intense and dedicated preparation (such as a conference, or a special subject), the honorarium ought to reflect that. As we shall see below, the preacher's gifts, experience, expertise and other such factors make a difference in how he might be honoured, and the same is true for the visiting preacher. Equally, the size, wealth and position of the church he visits, or other environmental or circumstantial factors, should have some impact on the way he is remunerated. If nothing else, it is generally (though not always) more exhausting to preach nine sermons in three days to five hundred people than it is to preach two sermons on one day to fifty people.

Taking stock

To return to our main thread, there are a number of particular duties and opportunities that belong to gospel ministers, as well as more generic concerns, of which a church might wish to take account. It may be that there are some particular allowances that the government makes for ministers of the gospel, perhaps with regard to taxation or housing. No church or pastor is obliged to take these up, but it might be foolish not to do so for as long as they are offered, and can be embraced without compromise. In many situations, there may be organisations or advisers and accountants who can help churches and elders to make the most of such advantages.

In addition, and—again—depending on the country and the culture, a church may wish to consider other provision for the pastor and other elders, some of which we have already hinted at above. A pastor's library is his toolbox and his medicine cabinet: can the church provide an annual or monthly book budget that allows him to purchase the volumes and subscriptions that he most needs? What about conferences and fellowships that feed his soul and inform his thinking and stir his affections and direct his will and equip him for service? What about his travel to and from such conferences, not to mention the other travel by road or rail, or even air or sea, that might be involved in his daily or occasional business? Are there computer equipment or office stationery requirements for the work that he does? What about communications technology that he uses entirely or primarily in the service of Christ and his church? He gives hospitality, no doubt, out of his general resources, but is he ever required to 'entertain' in a more distinct way? Many of these provisions should typically be considered not as part of the salary, but as proper benefits alongside of it. If they are, for some reason, rolled up as part of the salary, then they ought not simply to be swallowed up and lost sight of in the blur of the whole.

Once again, what of his health and his future, and that of his family, under God? The church might consider providing for possible medical needs. Depending on the circumstances, it could do this by way of medical insurance, or by an arrangement in which emergencies might be addressed or help given when required. What about sick leave? If the pastor is laid aside briefly, or struck down with a longer-term affliction, how and for how long will the church take care of him and his family? What about imprisonment? In some environments, this must be taken into account. Will the church take care of the man's family and property, as necessary, should he be incarcerated?

What about old age and death? Suppose a man serves for many years in a particular place and is no longer able to serve as he once did. Perhaps he must relinquish the pastoral office, or make a transition to a less demanding role, because of advancing age, declining capacity or ill health. Has the church provided adequately for his retirement, whatever form that might take or for whatever reason it might come about? It may be that the church has been paying into a pension, or providing a salary that enables a man to pay into his own pension. Other churches might be able to provide a regular sum (perhaps an annual amount) which the pastor is free to invest towards retirement.

A church might continue paying the man a salary—even a reduced one—after his retirement, if it has not been able to prepare beforehand. I know of one scandalous situation in which a dear man of God, and a faithful labourer in his harvest field, was wealthier on his British state pension after the formal age of retirement than he had ever been while 'fully supported' as the pastor of any of the churches he served. Under the circumstances, that was an act of wickedness on the part of the churches involved. Brothers, these things ought not to be!

The same consideration should be made of missionaries. Many of them live and die in the place where the Lord and his church have sent them. Others, because of changing circumstances, health concerns, family demands or other realities of life, might eventually return to their earthly home country or another place of relative ease. And what then? Are they to be forgotten because the glamour of 'the mission field' no longer attaches to them and the aura of visible sacrifice no longer hangs upon them? By no means! Again, care should be taken that they continue to receive what is needful.

But what if a minister dies and leaves a young family behind? To what extent would the church care for them? What sort of provision should be made unless or until his widow might remarry? What if he dies in harness and leaves an elderly widow? To be sure, 'if anyone does not provide for his own, and especially for those of his household, he has denied the faith and is worse than an unbeliever' (1 Tim. 5:8). Nevertheless, there may be circumstances in which the church should take responsibility for the care of a pastor's widow, especially if she too has served well, and if her circumstances mean that others are not in a position to care for her. It would be a travesty of justice and of mercy if, after serving Christ and his church, such a woman were left to fall on the charity of others.

House and home

Neither should we forget the question of housing. Typically, it is best for the shepherd of the sheep to live among those whom he seeks to shepherd, both in terms of gathering a flock and guiding and guarding the flock so gathered. Ideally, he would usefully be in the community where the church meets. What does that mean? Different cultures may impose different expectations or demands. In some places, that requires a much more significant financial investment. The church and the man have various ways to address this.

For some, it may be the provision of a manse or other church accommodation for the man who serves. If that is the case, then the church must also ask where and how the man will live should he move or, for some reason, step down or retire from office. Perhaps a church can righteously provide a loan which enables the minister to purchase a property and pay back the loan at a reasonable rate? Others might find a friend within the church itself, or another wealthy Christian, who is willing to part-purchase a home as an investment. A Christian might own an appropriate property that he or she rents to the pastor at a reasonable rate, taking any financial 'hit' as part of their own contribution to the work of the ministry.

A pastor who is a single man, or a pastor and his wife without children, might enjoy accommodation in the home of another member with a larger property, if that can be done righteously. It may be that a gift will enable the pastor to purchase a home, or at least make the necessary down payment. It may be that he moves from a richer or more expensive area to a poorer and cheaper one, and is able to buy outright where he could only rent or pay a mortgage before—that might liberate a church. It may be that the congregation or members in it can build or supply a house.

The church might pay a salary that—in keeping with other principles—allows the man to purchase a house or rent an appropriate property (making an assessment of the right use of funds, and appreciating the conviction which some have that a mortgage is a debt that is unconscionable). In that case, two churches of identical size and financial health, each with the same healthy esteem for a man and his ministry, but at opposite ends of a country, or one in a rural and one in an urban environment, might pay salaries that—on the outside—seem radically different. However, this reflects the fact that housing in one place is four or five times more expensive than in the other.

In every instance, proper consideration should be given to the size of the pastor's family, the demands of hospitality, the need for space to study, and other such matters. We are not saying that a pastor needs a mansion in an upmarket part of town, nor that he should live in a dingy and cramped property, even if most of the members do. But, in a church of mansion dwellers, the pastor ought not to be in a hut; in a church of cottage dwellers, the pastor needs no palace. In general, and in times of greater peace and prosperity (for the situation may be radically different in times of persecution), the servant of God should be able to live competently and comfortably, at an appropriate level, in keeping with the place in which, and the people whom, he serves.

Churches should also take into account the fact of inflation in the economy. If the cost of living increases by, say, 3% annually, then a salary that is fixed over the course of five or seven years might quickly slide from reasonably generous to genuinely austere. Some pastors find themselves enjoying what would have been a generous wage had they been serving fifty years previously, simply because the church has failed to keep up to date.

No fixed formula

We should avoid hard-and-fast formulae in this matter: different situations, different cultures, different national and local economies, different family dynamics ... all of these things should be taken into account. Think of particular family circumstances; take into account local tax structures; consider the cost of housing in a particular place; assess the typical cost of living at a reasonable level. All must be taken into consideration.

Some advocate paying a man the average wage earned by the congregation, or the average wage of the country or region in which the church is situated.

Others try to peg pastoral salaries to another easily identifiable scale, such as a professional teacher's salary. While these may be helpful points of reference, they should not be the final determinant. In the case and circumstances of a man like Spurgeon, he reached an arrangement with the deacons that he would receive the pew rents from the church. When the congregation increased to several thousands, he continued to be granted that privilege, but promptly gave most of it away as it came in, regardless of the amount he was receiving. Each case must be judged on its merits.

For example, considered as a whole, pastors ought to be among the most competent men in the congregation, and that ought to have implications for the way that we assess their worth. Of course, competence in one sphere might be very different from competence in another, with its associated rewards. For example, a competent business owner might still obtain far higher material rewards than a competent teacher.

Or, suppose we decided to peg ministerial salary to another professional scale. How do we compare the two? Without seeking to denigrate or undermine the labours of any other profession, or the importance of their role, we must guard against reaching the conclusion that this is the most suitable means of establishing a pastoral salary. How does one assess or compare the pastor's roles and responsibilities with those of a secular profession? What kinds of demands are placed on the pastor and the job to which his is being compared?

What if one takes into account performance-related pay within a given profession, or progress within a particular field, or the range of pay scales that might characterise a particular job? How does one take into account the faithful discharge of pastoral labour over many years? One hopes that a pastor serving faithfully will gain wisdom and insight and experience; our Bibles require that we recognise that. How does one measure the particular gifts and capacities of a particular pastor? What difference would it make if you had a very inexperienced but unusually gifted man? How might one account for that?

An older, more experienced man should have that taken into account when his salary is being set—this factor should weigh more than with a younger man, however gifted. If there were several vocational elders of different gifts, graces, ages, experience, fruitfulness, recognised ability and so on, would or should they all be paid equally? I suggest not; at least, not necessarily. The assessment must be made on the basis of their ruling well (or not) and being worthy (or not) of double honour, taking into account all the relevant factors. A young, gifted, useful servant of God, whose capacities are publicly recognised, might be given equal or greater financial 'honour' when compared with an older man who has served without manifest distinction but with enduring faithfulness. Or it may be that the church considers the older man's proven faithfulness as having greater value than or equal value to the young man's developing fruitfulness. On the other hand, two men, of similar age, serving alongside each other with comparable gifts, graces, success and public recognition, might be equally rewarded.

Putting it into practice

So, how could a church go about addressing this? What is the righteous course of action with regard to pastoral remuneration? Are we acting according to biblical principle, or has pragmatism or expedience become the rule, perhaps by default? If a correction in our thinking and doing requires acting in faith, that should not hinder us if the thing itself is right. It may even be that a church, thinking through these things for itself, reaches the conclusion that it cannot alter things materially at this point in its history. However, they might approach the whole matter in a healthier way and on better principles. Bear in mind that there may be other principles (different kingdom investments, for example, or a sort of thoughtless pegging of a new pastor's salary to the previous man's wage) which might suggest an immediate or staged decrease in the level of remuneration. The problem may not lie so much with the sum of payment, but with the principles underlying that payment. This is often what needs to change. If, in the future, more money became available, a church might then say that it has reached a position in which it is both willing and able to demonstrate financially its principled assessment.

Let me therefore suggest three simple directions from which a church should consider the question, three measures that should be taken into account.

1. Righteous entitlement

First, looking from below, a church should consider the matter of righteous entitlement. What is the man entitled to receive in terms of his high calling and his personal circumstances, with the unavoidable demands and inherent expectations of the work he does in the place in which he is called to do it? This sets, at the very least, the bottom of the bracket. Remember again that this is not an act of charity but a proper recognition and reward of labour carried out.

2. Righteous assessment

Then, looking from the side, a church should consider

the matter of righteous assessment. What is the church able to provide? What is its capacity for principled support and generous supply? Are there particular circumstances, needs or opportunities in the life and ministry of the man, in the context of that particular work, that might require or demand a certain level of investment? This helps to establish in a sober-minded and realistic fashion a reasonable range within which the church should be working.

3. Righteous recognition and reward

Finally, looking from above, a church should consider the matter of righteous reward. This is a recognition of faithfulness, a thankful acknowledgment of fruitfulness, an appreciation of grace and gift in the under-shepherd, either in the bud or the bloom. How can the church show its esteem of the work and the worker? This pushes the church to think in terms of how or in what ways it can righteously recognise particular service, effort or achievement.

6
Thinking more widely

Every gospel church needs to take account of this challenge. It is an issue for existing and well-established churches, and a question for newly planted churches. It may bring a particular challenge for independent churches, especially if a spirit of isolationism has crept in among them. It may shake up a connection of churches of whatever denomination which has lost sight of the issue in the long-term, regular administration of church business. It might place particular demands on longer-established or more wealthy churches, and bring particular questions for poorer or smaller congregations.

Sending and supporting

When churches are planted in accordance with biblical principles, it is possible, even likely, that initial support will come from outside, from a sending or supporting church. It seems likely that when Paul was first sent out from Antioch they assumed responsibility for taking care of their emissary. However, as—Lord willing—the seed is sown and a church begins to grow and become more firmly established, the expectation is that the church should seek to become self-supporting.

The goal ought to be not so much mere financial independence (a first step, certainly!) but rather financial freedom. We should hope and work for a level of financial support that quickly allows for the planted church's own investment in gospel endeavour, sustaining itself, advancing its immediate scope, and investing in the spread of the gospel and the planting of churches in other places, either independently or in cooperation with others. So we see that it is not long in the New Testament record before churches that Paul has planted are themselves engaged in supporting him and assisting in the planting or relief of other churches, including those that might originally have been considered 'mother churches'. Indeed, some were impoverishing themselves for the sake of the gospel.

In practice, perhaps a sending or supporting

church might offer a number of years of full financial provision, allowing for the initial labour to take place without concern for financial support. Perhaps, once the congregation is established and growing, support from that other church or churches might reduce at a flat rate of 20% or 25% per year, so that within four or five years the church is expected and, Lord willing, able to support itself. Of course, such a scheme presumes that pastoral priorities within the fledgling church reflect the kinds of focus we have just described.

A church might support an evangelist sent into a country or region for the entirety of his ministry, while presuming that local men raised up to the pastorate will be supported by local churches. If a church is formed from existing believers in an area, then this matter of ministerial support is one that ought to be carefully considered as part of the process. All this presumes that each situation should be considered on a case-by-case basis, for there is no absolute rule in these matters, and some churches may advance more quickly, while others may take years of investment to get off the ground.

Bear in mind that many churches in richer or more stable countries have unusual scope for assisting pastors in poorer, more troubled or less-developed countries, or those with a significantly lower cost of living. For what would barely scratch the surface of a full pastoral salary in Western Europe or the US, for example, we might be able fully to support a pastor in a developing nation. There may be a richer city church that can help a poorer rural cause. At the very least, grants of books or assistance with housing could easily be provided for needy men. Of course, there are dangers even here. Cultivating a handout mentality, allowing poorer churches in poorer places or nations to neglect their own duties, overlooking the sacrificial demands of supporting ministers near at hand—all of these things must be taken into account. However, neither laziness on the part of the giver nor pride on the part of the receiver should make the richer church overlook or neglect the opportunities to minister to others that the Lord provides.

Cooperation between churches

And what of cooperation between existing churches? I recall a situation several years ago which involved five churches, all within one or two hours' drive of each other, and all struggling with evangelising in their communities. In each case, it seemed that there was a felt lack of ability or time, or desire or even will to make Christ known. The difficulties of performing this duty were in danger of becoming excuses not to do so. In a couple of instances, the churches only had one pastor or were beginning to decline.

One suggestion made was that the various churches, while they still had the opportunity, should seek to identify a man from among them with a gift for evangelistic endeavour. Those churches might each contribute a fifth of that man's support. While remaining under the care of one particular church and her elders, through whom also his support would be channelled, he might visit each of the five communities on the same day of each week in succession. This would give each of the five churches a sustained and dedicated evangelistic presence in its immediate neighbourhood. In addition, he might preach in each of the churches in some kind of rotation, so lightening the preaching load especially of the sole elders in some of those congregations. I do not believe the counsel was taken.

In our own experience as a church, we knew of a couple of men in recently planted congregations who did not have full financial support. We were given the opportunity to support a man for a day a week. That man would come to our community for that day and help us to reach out with the good news of the Lord Christ. In return, we helped him, and the church of which he was a part, to keep him wholly concentrated on the work of the kingdom to which he had been set apart. In another case, a church not quite able to support its own pastor had a more adequate salary made up with the help of a number of like-minded churches willing to 'chip in' for the sake of the gospel.

Historically, the Particular Baptists were known for cooperating in the sending out of evangelists to areas of the United Kingdom in which the gospel was not being preached, or assisting sister churches. The same spirit of mutual endeavour would serve us well today. We are, perhaps, a little slow in considering avenues of service in which a little Christian inventiveness would give us greater scope for gospel investment.

That is the case not only in seeking to win new converts, but also in ministering to those already called out of the world to Christ. In the United Kingdom, there are many towns and villages, and some cities, that have smaller and struggling congregations. They are, in some cases, doctrinally faithful, and spiritually viable, but financially limited. What can be done? What if a church identifies a man who might prove an effective pastor-evangelist to revitalise such a church, under God, but which cannot afford even a subsistence salary? Or what if, despite the faithful efforts of a godly pastor (not just someone who is trying to manage the church to a quiet death!), progress is slow, and the church begins to struggle to support that man?

Asking and answering

The burden in such cases does not lie simply with other churches to intervene, but also with the church in difficulty to seek an answer. We must accept that, in this world, some will be poor, and some will be poorer than others. We must accept that some churches will not be able to provide for their pastors to the same extent as others. All this is true and reasonable. However, at the very least, the financially struggling church (which may well be struggling in other spheres as well) can and should bring its need to the attention of sister churches. Even if these churches cannot do more than pray, they can do that—they can join with the struggling church in calling on the Lord of heaven and earth to provide all that is needful for his people. But one or more churches might also prove God's means of bringing the needed blessing to that congregation—not only prayerful but also financial support, together with other practical contributions to and investments in the work of the gospel in a particular place. Perhaps one or more churches, better provided for, can help the church support the struggling pastor. If there is no preacher in the place, perhaps other congregations can send someone in to serve, and support them in doing so.

It could be that, in some places, two smaller churches might join together in order to make a more proper investment in the work of the kingdom of Christ. Apart, they might be able to do little, with two streams of income each disappearing into the desert of building maintenance and visiting preachers. There are also some financial trusts or other charitable organisations and funds that may be available for investment in preaching the truth as it is in Jesus, either for churches or for ministers. These should not be overlooked.

Faith and hope

In these ways, struggling causes can be not only sustained but revitalised. City boroughs and districts, towns and their neighbourhoods, villages and hamlets, otherwise in danger of losing a vital gospel witness, might in this way continue to have the light of the gospel shining in them. In every such case, the concern can never be simply to maintain the *status quo* for a few more years. We cannot afford to labour with a sort of faithful hopelessness or hopeless faithfulness, applauding our orthodoxy while lamenting our impotence. The desire and expectation must be to preach the Word, in season and out of season, winning souls and strengthening saints for the work God has given us to do, for the glory of his name and the blessing of his church.

In each case, in any case, in every case, the point is to step back and ask: Have we made a principled, biblical, righteous assessment as to what the Word of God demands with regard to a particular church of Christ, or any one of the elders of Christ's church? How should we support the work of the kingdom of our Lord? We must ask the right questions with regard to pastoral support: What are they entitled to as a matter of righteousness? In terms of our stewardship, what can we afford as a matter of righteousness? How can we recognise 'ruling well' and being 'worthy of double honour' and reward it as a matter of righteousness?

Consider your ways

When we consider such matters as these, some churches and some Christians may need to face the question that the Lord brought to his people of old through the prophet Haggai: 'Is it time for you yourselves to dwell in your panelled houses, and this temple to lie in ruins?' (Hag. 1:4). The Lord of hosts challenged his people with the consequences of their confused and carnal priorities: 'Consider your ways! You have sown much, and bring in little; you eat, but do not have enough; you drink, but you are not filled with drink; you clothe yourselves, but no one is warm; and he who earns wages, earns wages to put into a bag with holes' (Hag. 1:5–6). Could it be that some of the declension and difficulty that some of us face is because we have not, in our kingdom endeavours, always put our money where our mouth is? Have we pandered ourselves while neglecting the building of the temple of living stones, the church of Christ through the preaching of the Word of God?

They were not the only people to hear God's warnings and receive God's assurances. He spoke also through Malachi:

> 'Will a man rob God? Yet you have robbed Me! But you say, "In what way have we robbed You?" In tithes and offerings. You are cursed with a curse, for you have robbed Me, even this whole nation. Bring all the tithes into the storehouse, that there may be food in My house, and try Me now in this,' says the LORD of hosts, 'if I will not open for you the windows of heaven and pour out for you such blessing that there will not be room enough to receive it' (Mal. 3:8–10).

I am not so foolish as to suggest that a reformation of our personal and church finances alone will invariably bring an immediate upturn in spiritual fortunes, but neither am I so foolish as to imagine that the Lord overlooks the way in which we order our financial affairs as churches and as Christians. If, as some have suggested, the last part of a man to be converted is his wallet, perhaps it is time to consider whether or not we have, as so often and in so many ways, deprived ourselves of the blessings that the Lord holds out to his faithful people.

Heavenly priorities

Our financial priorities are a reflection of our spiritual priorities. Who or what has the firstfruits? Could it not be the time to try the Lord in these things? Should we not bring our tithes and our offerings into his storehouse, that there may be food in his house, and then look for the windows of heaven to open and blessings to pour out in such a manner that we barely know what to do with them?

Fundamentally, our answers to these questions are a register of our esteem of Christ and his Word. Our capacity might lag behind our intention, and our ability behind our motives, but our intentions and motives should reflect the high view we have of the ministry of God's truth in the church of Christ's love. Faithful churches and pastors know that, ultimately, the true rewards are the eternal ones.

Every Christian, whether giving or receiving, is looking forward to the day when he or she hopes to hear those precious words, 'Well done, good and faithful servant; you were faithful over a few things, I will make you ruler over many things. Enter into the joy of your lord' (Matt. 25:21, 23). That is what finally matters. So a man might live poor and die early in the service of his Lord, only to enter into an eternal reward of unimaginable excellence. In doing so, he is no loser.

A thousand testimonies might be gathered to underscore the fact that no-one ever suffered the loss of anything worth losing in the service of the best of Masters. A multitude of additional trails of evidence might be employed to underline the fact that to serve Christ in this world does often mean pain and poverty. A faithful pastor and preacher signs up knowing that this is the case, and ready to seek the grace to humble himself under whatever circumstances his faithfulness puts upon him. And yet it remains the fact that the labourer is worthy of his hire.

Before Christ, before the saints and before the world, our support of our pastors and our investment in the ministry of God's holy Word, financially and in a hundred other ways, testifies to our true values. Let it never be said of us that we dishonoured the Lord who gives gifts to his church, despised the gifts themselves, discouraged the saints, and confirmed the disdainful and dismissive expectations of God's enemies. Rather, let our financial investments in the kingdom of God, and in those who have a distinct service in that kingdom, testify that we are working in and waiting for that city which has everlasting foundations, the city which cannot be shaken, whose builder and maker is God.

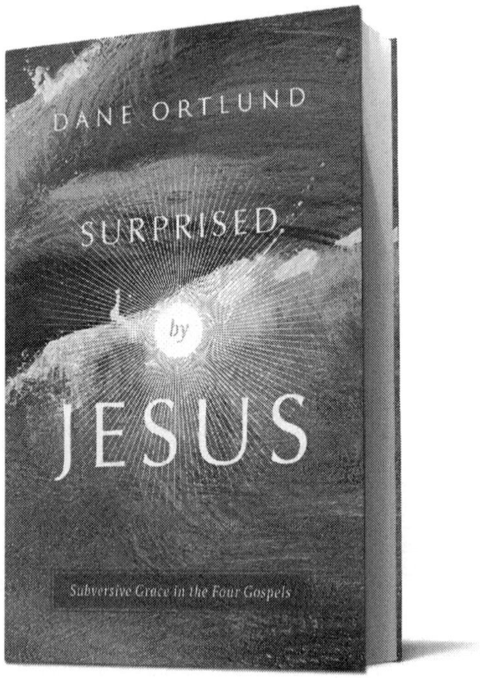
DANE ORTLUND
SURPRISED
by
JESUS
Subversive Grace in the Four Gospels